THIS BOOK

Unde

your reactions

to trauma

a guide for survivors of trauma and their families

Revised Version

by **Dr Claudia Herbert,** BSc(Hons), MSc, DClin Psy, AFBPsS

Chartered Clinical Psychologist

UKCP Registered Cognitive Behavioural Psychotherapist

EMDR Consultant

Foreword by Dr David Grand, Ph.D., EMDR Facilitator, New York

The phenomenon of global terrorism has brought the existence of trauma, its symptoms and its treatments to greater public consciousness. It is in such a climate that "Understanding Your Reactions to Trauma - A guide for survivors of trauma and their families," becomes such a valuable resource for us all. The book is written clearly and concisely, which makes it highly understandable for the general public. It is however, also a valuable resource for anyone in the health field including doctors, nurses, social workers and all others who care for and heal others.

The existence of trauma is not new. It has slipped in and out of public consciousness after every major war, natural and man-made disaster. It is our difficulty in admitting and facing trauma and its after effects that so often leads us to ignore or deny its existence. In the past trauma, treatments were lengthy and relatively ineffective. Now, state-of-the-art treatments like EMDR (Eye Movement Desensitization and Reprocessing), which I use actively in my practice, can effectively relieve the condition of PTSD (Post Traumatic Stress Disorder), frequently within only a few treatment sessions.

"Understanding Your Reactions to Trauma - A guide for survivors of trauma and their families," provides both hope and help for sufferers of trauma and those who surround them. It is a source book, which guides trauma survivors to recognize and understand the cluster of their trauma symptoms and their causes, and to discover the paths to recovery and reconnection with themselves, mind body and spirit as well as their families and communities. It contains simple guidance for self-recognition and self-support for those who have been exposed to traumatic circumstances.

"Understanding Your Reactions to Trauma - A guide for survivors of trauma and their families," contains two resource sections. The first section lists the available literature on the topic of trauma and the second section provides guidance on how to find therapeutic help for individuals affected by trauma for those residing in every English speaking country.

This book is comprehensive and useful, practical and informative. Due to the widespread nature of traumatic experiences and their aftermath, "Understanding Your Reactions to Trauma - A guide for survivors of trauma and their families," is a resource that deserves to find its way into every home, library and health setting.

Introduction to the Revised Edition

Seven years have passed since this booklet was first written. Much has happened since then. The world has seen a number of major catastrophes and disasters and this booklet has been translated into several other languages to help people in different parts of the world to understand their often overwhelming responses to trauma in order to enable them to start their own path towards healing.

For those of us working as therapists in the trauma field, we have also learned so much more and gained a far richer understanding and knowledge about the effects of trauma and how we might help people to recover. It therefore feels time to revise and update this booklet to bring it up to our current knowledge.

Changes that have been made to this revised edition include, a general update to our latest knowledge about trauma memories and their effect, a new chapter on coping with safety behaviours, a new chapter on chronic pain, latest knowledge about effective trauma treatment methods and a complete update of resources. Additionally the booklet has been changed so that it will now be suitable for all English speaking countries and listing of contact addresses are available for different countries.

The purpose of the booklet remains the same. It is intended to inform and guide people, to increase their understanding of reactions that often feel so out of control. The aim is through clear information to give back some control so that those affected will feel less isolated and be better equipped to seek out the help that they may need.

Recent research in Oxford[1] with 42 people suffering from Post-Traumatic Stress Disorder (or PTSD for short) after different traumatic experiences has shown that people found the booklet very helpful in supporting them alongside their course of therapy for PTSD. They also indicated that they would have found it helpful if they had been given the booklet as soon as they were fit enough to read it after the trauma and if copies of the booklet were available in all doctor's waiting rooms. They felt that the booklet helped them to feel that their reactions were understandable and common after trauma and that they were not alone in their suffering. The same feedback was given from survivors of the Turkish earthquake in 1999, who read this booklet.

This booklet has not been written for and is not intended as a replacement for specialist trauma therapy. Research in Oxford[2] with 50 people who had been traumatized by road traffic accidents has shown that the booklet does not work as an independent tool to effectively heal PTSD. For that purpose, references to more comprehensive self-help books and also information on how to look for the right form of therapy will be provided.

([1]Herbert, C., Ehlers, A., Clark, D.M., Fennell, M., Hackmann, A. & McManus, F. - in preparation)

([2]Herbert, C., Ehlers, A., Clark, D.M., Fennell, M., Hackmann, A. & McManus, F. - in preparation)

Acknowledgements

Much appreciation is extended to Dr Joan Kirk, Head of the Adult Clinical Psychology Department at the Warneford Hospital in Oxford, for encouraging me to pursue my idea of a trauma booklet and for supervising its growth. I would also like to thank my former supervisor, Christine Küchemann, Principal Psychologist at the Adult Clinical Psychology Department at the Warneford Hospital in Oxford, for her thoughtful editing and for being there whenever I needed her support. I am much indebted to Dr James Thompson, under whose thorough supervision and supportive guidance I gained my first clinical experiences in this field at the Traumatic Stress Clinic in London and who has been influential in shaping my understanding of trauma.

Special thanks go to Ann Wetmore, at Mount Saint Vincent University in Halifax, Canada, for her belief in me and her openness and encouragement throughout the time that I have known her and for her helpful comments during the writing of the preliminary version of this booklet. I am also thankful to the many other colleagues who have supported me throughout the different stages of this project. Dr Gillian Butler, Alison Croft, Caroline Cupitt, Dr John Hall, Martina Müller, Kate Rosen, Linette Whitehead, Debbie Wint and David Westbrook are just a few names from the long list of those who gave their support. I am grateful to the Oxfordshire and East Anglia Regional Health Authority who provided the funding for the research project, on which this booklet is based.

My gratitude is also extended to Nigel Newbery for all his help with the imaginative design work, which greatly enhances the readability of the booklet.

The first version of this guide grew out of a two-year research project with trauma survivors, during which the booklet underwent various stages of a consultation and evaluation process. I am deeply thankful to all trauma survivors who provided their input to this guide in order to help others that may be suffering in similar ways as a result of a trauma.

For this revised edition, I would like to additionally thank Professor Anke Ehlers, Professor David Clark, Professor Richard Mayou, , Dr Melanie Fennell, Ann Hackman, Dr Freda McManus and Doç Mehmet Sungur, who have kindly supported the booklet's incorporation into their own research for further evaluation. I would also like to thank Dr Mike Hobbs for initiating this idea. This research has helped to further clarify this booklet's purpose as a very helpful guide to understanding reactions to trauma.

Finally, I would like to thank all the numerous other professionals, Uschi May and my clients for directly or indirectly contributing to aspects of the knowledge contained in this booklet. I would also like to express my gratitude to Ulf Jarisch, as without his support, I may not for a long time have made the space to write this revision. Last, but not least, my appreciation and love goes to my own family for supporting me with the revision of this guide.

Contents

		page
Foreword		2
Introduction to the Revised Edition		3
Acknowledgements		4
Preface		6

Part 1: understanding trauma and your reactions to it

1.1	Introduction	12
1.2	What is a trauma?	14
1.3	Who is this guide written for?	17
1.4	Why can a trauma have such a big psychological effect on you?	19
1.5	How do people make sense of and adjust to a trauma?	22
1.6	The most common ways of reacting to trauma	23
	Re-experiencing the trauma	24
	Numbing and avoidance reactions	28
	Reactions of increased arousal	32
1.7	Other reactions to trauma	38
	Reactions linked to loss of a person close to you	38
	Physical disfigurement/loss of parts of your body	39
	Chronic Pain	39
	Sexual difficulties	40
	Depression	41
	Guilt/self-blame	42
1.8	What is Post-Traumatic Stress Disorder (PTSD)?	44
1.9	Why don't all people react in the same way to trauma?	47

Part 2: coping with the trauma

2.1	The process of re-building your life	50
2.2	Some things that might help you start with your process of recovery	52
	Getting it out – working it through!	53
	Ways of talking through the trauma	55
	Tackling avoidance	56
	Coping with safety behaviours	59
	Coping with anxiety	60
	Coping with anger or irritability	63
	Sleeping problems	64
	Sexual difficulties	65
	Alcohol and drugs	67
	Medication	68
2.3	How to get professional help	70
2.4	If you are in therapy, stay with it – don't give up too soon!	75
2.5	Effect on your family or partner	76
2.6	Further reading	77
2.7	Contact addresses	81

Epilogue		84

Preface

Confidentiality

In order to enhance understanding and readability this booklet contains some examples. The names and personal details of all persons featuring in the examples have been changed in order to maintain confidentiality. Any resemblance to real life names or circumstances is therefore coincidental.

Rationale for a booklet on trauma

The last thing that you probably feel like doing right now is to read a book on trauma. This is really very understandable. You probably want to do everything possible to get away from the trauma that you have experienced. However, getting away may make you feel a little better in the short term, but it won't actually resolve the feelings and problems that may have arisen for you as a result of your trauma in the long-term. This book has therefore been written to help you understand what goes on when you have been in a trauma and how to get over it. It is based on the belief that the more you understand about your reactions to trauma, the more in control and able you will feel to actively find ways to help you with your recovery and healing.

This book has been written for you as an incentive to do something that will help you move on and enable you to re-claim your Self and your life as best as you can.

How to read this booklet

Reading is often not an easy task while you are in the midst of coming to terms with a trauma. Your levels of concentration may be low and you may find it hard to stick at it. **As this booklet contains quite a lot of material, here are some ways which might help you to make use of the booklet:**

- First skim over the booklet and familiarize yourself with its format and content.

- Notice any bits of text that may stand out for you and if you feel like reading these try and do so.

- You may find that reading the booklet in small steps and for a few minutes at a time is much easier than trying to read it from back to front.

- Don't be put off by any words that you might not understand. Just ignore them and read those bits that make sense to you.

- If there are parts that upset you it is probably because they remind you of your own trauma. It can be hard to feel your own upset, but this is not dangerous. It won't make your trauma any worse. Allow yourself to feel your upset, nurture and soothe yourself while you are feeling this. It can often be a real relief to express your feelings and very healing.

- Not all parts may feel relevant to you. This is fine. Read those parts that you feel relate to you most. If you feel like it you could read some of the other parts a different time to find out if they contain some bits that may also be helpful to you.

- If reading is a real problem for you, you may find it helpful for someone to read this booklet with you. Chose a person who you feel would be understanding and patient. It might help you to go over those bits together that haven't been entirely clear to you several times.

- If you can't find another person to read with you then you could read the booklet aloud onto a tape, CD or minidisk. Don't try and understand it while you are reading it out loud. Go over it afterwards by listening to it. That way you can go over parts again and again, without actually having to read them yourself.

Cautions

Reading a booklet about the reactions to trauma may be quite difficult for you. Some of the examples may remind you of aspects of your own trauma and you may find yourself becoming distressed when you read these. As described before, feeling your distress can be very helpful to you even if it is a bit uncomfortable because you may not be so used to expressing it. It is often the start of a normal healing process.

However, if you feel that your levels of distress are unduly high and feel very overwhelming and uncontrollable put the booklet aside. Try and do something very different to distract yourself.

Also stop reading the booklet and do something different if any of the following occur:

- Feelings that you are losing touch with reality, such as experiencing extreme and overwhelming memories of the event, flashbacks, hallucinations
- If you experience very strong anxiety reactions, such as hyperventilation or panic attacks or an irregular heartbeat
- If you experience very strong bodily reactions, such as extensive shaking, feelings of extreme coldness or very hot flushes
- If you feel suicidal
- If you feel like wanting to harm yourself or others around you
- If you experience uncontrollable anger or rage

If you do experience any of these responses when you are reading this booklet you should discuss these with your Family Doctor or therapist before continuing to read this booklet.

Part 1

understanding trauma and your reactions to it

Part 1

1.1 Introduction

Sudden, traumatic life events can shatter people's lives. They can have a profound effect on the way that people feel about themselves and others and the nature of the world around them. People can experience utter confusion and often terror about the way they are feeling and behaving after a sudden traumatic event.

Harry who had survived a serious housefire said to me: *"After I had survived the actual trauma I thought it was all over – but it was then when it all really began." For many months he was unable to get images of the traumatic event out of his mind. Harry told me: "It was as if every day parts of the trauma were happening again. I wanted to put it behind me, to move on with my life, but it was as if the trauma wouldn't let me. Worse still, not only were my days filled with terrifying reminders of what had happened to me but even when I tried to get some rest from it through sleep at night it wouldn't leave me. I was haunted by repeated, recurring nightmares which seemed so real that I often woke up screaming and crying, convinced that I was on fire again. Whatever I did, it felt at the time that I just couldn't move forward but was totally trapped with the event. It felt so real that I was convinced at the time that I was going mad."*

Many people have the same or very similar reactions and fears as Harry. **People's reactions and responses after a trauma often feel so strong and overwhelming that it is not uncommon for people to feel that they are 'going mad' or 'losing complete control over their life'.** People are often surprised and relieved when they hear that they are not unique in experiencing these feelings – that they are not 'going mad' but that their reactions are common and understandable responses to trauma. Moreover, these can be helped and people can heal and recover from the trauma.

By talking through and working on specific aspects of the trauma (often in therapy) people are able to regain control over their lives and they are able to start to see light again, where they experienced mainly darkness before.

This booklet is intended as a starting point. It is intended as a guide to help you understand the various reactions and feelings that you are experiencing, in order to try and help shed some light on the various places of 'darkness' and uncertainty that you may be experiencing. Through this understanding you may find the confidence and courage within yourself to continue the process of working through your trauma. If you have not done so already, the booklet may also give you the courage to find and share your feelings with a person who can offer you more specialist help to aid with your process of recovery. This booklet is not intended as a replacement for psychological therapy or counselling but may help and enhance the effectiveness of this. A list of organizations that can help you find a therapist is provided under contact addresses at the back of this guide.

The process of recovery takes time and is unique to each person.

1.2 What is a trauma?

Although during your life you experience many situations which can be very stressful not many of these are real traumas.

Here is an example of a trauma:

'On Friday, 2nd July 1991, Sue leaves her work at the bank at about 5.00pm. It is a clear and pleasantly warm summer evening. As Sue is driving home in her blue Ford Montego with her colleague, Pamela, they are thinking ahead to the weekend. It had been a busy week and they are both looking forward to a relaxing time off work. Pamela is telling Sue that she is looking forward to playing with her three-year-old son that evening. As they approach a sharp bend in the road, Sue slows down. Suddenly, she sees Pamela lift her arms and hears her scream: "Stop, stop....Oh no!". Sue sees a car coming at high speed out of the bend, swerving towards her side of the road. She feels terrified and thinks: "This is it – I'm going to die!". Just then she hears an enormous bang, sounding almost like an explosion. Then there seems complete silence, which feels to Sue as if it is lasting endlessly long. Gradually, Sue becomes aware of a sharp pain on her nose, forehead and chest. It feels to Sue as if the seatbelt is pushing her down and she is unable to lift herself up. As she manages to turn her head to the side she sees Pamela lying slumped back in her seat, with blood trickling from her nose and from a large cut on her forehead. She hears Pamela saying: "You've been in an accident. Are you alive? Can you hear me Sue?"..... .'

There are many ways in which traumas can be defined. Usually, however, a person would have **'experienced, witnessed, or been confronted with an event or events that involve actual or threatened death or serious injury, or a threat to the physical integrity of oneself or others. The person's response would have involved intense fear, helplessness, or horror'**[1].

([1]This is a definition of trauma based on the definition used in the Diagnostic Statistical Manual IV of the American Psychiatric Association, 1994).

Both Sue and Pamela have experienced an event that **can be described as a trauma.** They have been in a road traffic accident. Both Sue and Pamela thought and felt that there was a real possibility that they might die during the accident. The accident therefore involved **threatened death and injury** (possibly serious injury) to both of them. They responded with **intense fear and horror** (on realizing that they were going to crash). They also felt **helpless** as they were unable to prevent the accident from happening.

For the purpose of this booklet, Sue and Pamela's story ends here. In reality, however, the rescue operation, the nature of the experiences in hospital, the reactions of professionals and those close to you and often also the resulting legal proceedings may be sources of further traumatization. Sometimes these can even be experienced as more than the initial traumatic event itself.

Other types of traumatic events

The above is an example of one type of specific trauma, a Road Traffic Accident. **There are many types of other specific traumas.** Some of these, like the Road Traffic Accident, which also includes accidents involving a motorbike or bicycle, may fall into the category of '**Man-made Disasters**'. '**Man-made**' means that the trauma happened because of a **human error or an error made by a machine or system,** which has been designed by humans. Some other examples of Man-made disasters include:

> **Transport Disasters,** such as Rail/Tube/Coach Disasters, such as the Paddington Train Crash in 2000 or the Selby Rail Disaster in 2001; **Air Disasters; Maritime Disasters,** such as the Zeebrugge Ferry Disaster in 1987; **Fires and Gas Explosions; Severe Electric Shocks,** such as through accidents on electric powerlines; **Building Collapses; Environmental Disasters,** such as a nuclear catastrophe or chemical spillage and others.

Natural disasters make up another category of trauma, examples of this include:

> **Earthquakes,** such as the Turkish earthquakes in 1999 or the Kobe earthquake in Japan in 1995; **Floods,** such as the floods in the Netherlands in 1995; **Storms,** such as in Southern Germany in 1999; **Forest Fires; Volcano Eruptions;** and others.

The third category of trauma are instances of **violence, crime and terror.** These would include:

Acts of Domestic Violence, such as physical abuse; Stabbings; Hold-ups and Robbery; Acts of Terrorism, such as the 11th September 2001 attack on the World Trade Centre in New York and the White House in Washington, DC; Shootings, such as the Shootings at a School in Dunblane in Scotland 1996 or the Shootings at a school in Erfurt, Germany in 2002; Bomb Explosions, such as the Omagh Bombing in 1998; Rape; Sexual Abuse; Acts of Inhumanity, such as Solitary Confinement and/or Torture; Wars, such as the Second World War, the Falklands Conflict, the Gulf War, the Civil War in the former Yugoslavia, and others.

Man-made traumas and traumas caused by instances of violence, crime and terror are often harder to adjust to and come to terms with than natural disasters. The above list is not complete but gives examples of the many events that could be traumatic experiences for people, who have been affected by them. Life events such as divorce, redundancy, miscarriage or stillbirth and sudden death of a loved person can also be traumatic events, depending on the particular circumstances in which these occurred.

1.3 Who is this guide written for ?

All categories and types of traumatic experiences can result in long-lasting emotional and other life difficulties. This guide is written especially for people who have experienced a trauma relating to a sudden, specific event. This would include large scale disasters and catastrophes as well as specific traumatic incidents, such as Road Traffic Accidents, Fires, Single acts of Violence, and others.

People who have experienced repeated and prolonged trauma (such as, for example, acts of long-lasting domestic violence or acts of inhumanity, such as torture), several traumas and early childhood traumas (such as childhood sexual and/or physical and/or severe emotional abuse) may also find parts of this booklet helpful. **However, the booklet is not comprehensive enough to address the effects that may result from such experiences. If you have experienced a prolonged trauma you should read more specialist books** (there is a list of some references to specific books at the back of this booklet). **You should also try to get help from a skilled professional who is trained to offer therapy for these more complex trauma problems.** Often the your doctor is a good starting point in finding out where such specialist help may be available. A supportive doctor who understands your difficulties may even be able to arrange specialist help for you.

Traumas can also have a devastating effect on children's well-being. Although children's feelings may be similar to those of adult trauma survivors, the way in which they are expressed can be very different from adults. Depending on their age at the time of the trauma children may not have enough knowledge of language to be able to talk about their distress. Instead they can show their feelings through unusual ways of behaving. It is very important not to underestimate the effect of traumatic experiences on children. **However, this booklet** has not been written for child survivors of trauma and parents are encouraged to find specialist help if they think their children may be affected by a traumatic experience.

As outlined earlier, this guide is not written to replace specialist help where needed but it may be helpful in conjunction to therapy. **This guide assumes that if you can understand your reactions to trauma as common, explainable responses and not as 'abnormal' or 'mad' or anything to be ashamed of, this will provide you with the basis for successful recovery from trauma.** It may also enable you to seek specialist help earlier rather than later, if you feel that this could be of benefit to you.

1.4 Why can a trauma have such a big psychological effect on you?

Although most people know through the media that traumas affect people all the time, most people believe that they are safe – that these things will not happen to them. Alternatively, you might have even imagined how you would cope if you were in a trauma like the one that you may have watched others going through on the television, for example. Most likely your thoughts would have been either that "this would be awful and you wouldn't know what to do!" or they may have been that you "would have reacted very differently had it been you in that situation!" Now that you are in a situation of having survived a trauma, you may feel confused because it all feels so different to how you previously thought it would be if you ever were in a trauma. It is as if all your previously held beliefs have been shattered and the sense of safety that you had has gone. This is because **traumatic experiences are usually so different from anything that most people have ever experienced in their life before.**

Traumas usually happen suddenly and unexpectedly. During most other new experiences in your life there is often some time to adjust to the change. Even when you are faced with very difficult life experiences (for example, having to undergo a major operation) there is often time for you to prepare yourself. Usually, the more time you have to get used to difficult life experiences and the more prepared you feel, the better you will be able to cope with the experience. That is because you will already have had time to change and adjust your expectations of life accordingly. **However, you don't plan a trauma! It usually happens completely unexpectedly and sudden.** Therefore when it happens, your whole system, consisting of the interplay between your mental, emotional and bodily functions, has to adjust rapidly and cope as best as it can under the circumstances. There often is no time for mental preparation on how to react and cope while it happens. Usually your body's survival system takes over. When you look back with hindsight, you might find that **the way in which your system made you act during your trauma is not the way you would have chosen to react under normal circumstances.** Often people therefore feel that the way in which they acted during a trauma doesn't make sense, because it just doesn't fit with their usual way of being. Therefore people often feel very unsettled and completely out of their own control as a result of a trauma. It often feels as if the bubble of safety has burst. **Everything feels different to how it was before.** (Exceptions to this are prolonged and repeated traumas, which are not covered by this booklet. Some specialist books on these are listed in the reference section at the back.)

The experience of trauma often confronts you very suddenly with the possibility of your own and/or other people's deaths. Your trauma might have even involved you witnessing another person's death, may be even somebody you were very close to. Confronting death, whether your own or another person's is one of the most difficult experiences in any person's life, even when there is time to prepare for it. Loss through death linked to trauma is so sudden that there is no time for preparation. It can give rise to feelings of extreme fear, terror and despair both during and after the trauma.

Our human system has special ways of coping with the intensity of these fear responses during trauma and these are now explained in some detail on the next pages.

1.5 How do people make sense of and adjust to a trauma?

Because there has usually been no time to prepare before, a person will have to make sense of the trauma after it has happened. Traumatic events are commonly very different from any of your previous beliefs and expectations. A traumatic experience is therefore like a totally new experience for which you have had no time to prepare and most of which must be worked through after the experience of the trauma.

The working through enables you to make sense of the experience and re-adjust your life accordingly. Successful recovery cannot take place until you have found a way of understanding your traumatic experience. Understanding in this sense does not mean that you will be able to find answers to all the questions that might have been thrown up for you by the trauma. Rather, it means finding a way of integrating the experience into your life so that living can continue despite the trauma. It is about regaining control of your life despite the trauma and the changes resulting from it.

Successful recovery from trauma will therefore involve the building of a new model of life – a model which includes the experience of the trauma and yet allows you to carry on and re-gain control over your life.

This process of recovery will involve a time of disruption, disorientation and restlessness. The length and intensity of this disruptive period will vary from person to person but many of the reactions experienced during this process are common to and shared by others who have experienced a trauma.

The next section will outline some of the most common ways of reacting to trauma. **These are your humanly system's ways of adjusting and trying to make sense of a sudden, unexpected traumatic life experience.**

1.6 The most common ways of reacting to trauma

The most common reactions to trauma fall into three groups.

As part of the working-through process, your reactions may vary between the first group, which are **intense, reliving experiences of the trauma** and the second group, which are **periods during which you will feel utterly numb and empty of all feelings and emotions.** Often these two ways of reacting follow each other closely and start soon after the trauma. Sometimes you may not experience any symptoms for several weeks or months until some trigger, such as an anniversary or a reminder of some aspects of the trauma, sets off memories. These re-experiencing and numbing reactions often, but not always, occur in cycles, following one another.

A third group of reactions are **increased arousal symptoms.** These can occur at any time and they may or may not be triggered by specific events. These reactions will now be further explained.

RE-EXPERIENCING THE TRAUMA

a. Repeated distressing recollections of the trauma

Re-experiencing reactions happen because your survival system stored the information of what went on during your actual experience of the trauma in parts of your memory in the brain. There was no time to really make sense of what was happening during the trauma and it all felt very dangerous and alarming to you. Therefore the information was stored so that you would later have a memory of it. The memory is there to protect you in the case of any similar danger happening again. While this is very useful if there is indeed still real danger of the same trauma happening again, it is not so useful if the danger is now over and you don't actually really need this protection any longer.

The most common re-experiencing reaction is the unwanted and distressing memory of all or parts of the trauma. This happens when you repeat the trauma or parts of it in your mind again and again. Paul who had survived a gas explosion, for example, described: *"Even when I was out of the house trying to distract myself by walking my dog thoughts and feelings of the trauma wouldn't leave me. At times it felt as if the trauma had become a permanent part of my life, although more than eight months had passed since it happened."*

During these recollections you may repeatedly experience feelings, thoughts or images that you had during the trauma. These can include feelings of fear, panic, anger, helplessness, sadness, horror, and others. You may experience 'pangs of emotion', which make you feel extremely upset and tearful. You may feel discomfort and often think about the way in which the trauma left you feeling vulnerable, and how it shattered your feelings of personal safety and your beliefs in a meaningful and orderly world. You may even re-experience images, sounds, smells, tastes and bodily feelings, like pain, that were part of your trauma. All these memories may be stored in ways that don't really connect to each other. It may feel to you as if these are almost like separate snapshots of a film.'

You may also be thinking about what would have happened if you had reacted differently during the trauma. When you think in this way you may feel guilt or shame or anger with yourself or others. These thoughts and feelings are a way of wishing that things had been different and indicate that you are still trying to make sense of and understand what happened.

b. Recurrent distressing dreams, nightmares and sleeplessness (insomnia)

You may have distressing dreams and nightmares. Paul, for example, described: *"There were times when I didn't want to go to sleep at night for fear of my nightmares. In my dreams, I went through the trauma again and again. Often things in my dreams turned out worse even than they had been during the actual trauma. My dreams seemed so real that even when I woke up it took me a long time until I knew this was not really happening to me again."*

Like Paul, **you may also feel scared to go to sleep in fear of the intensity of your nightmares.** You may shout or toss and turn or lash out in your sleep. Most frequently, the distressing dreams and nightmares are the night-time re-enactment of the trauma. They are a kind of night-time equivalent of the flashbacks (described below), which take place during the day. They are linked to your memory storage of the trauma, which may get activated to protect you even during your sleep. The sensations you experience are so strong because this is how they felt at the time of the trauma to your survival system. They can even trigger some chemical responses inside you, which make you sweat or your heart race, because this is your body's way of protecting you. Your dreams and nightmares are part of your process of working through the trauma. **They are not dangerous!** However, they can feel especially disturbing because other systems, which during the day can help you to control these experiences may rest and shut down at night and therefore your nightmares or bad dreams may feel really out of control to you.

Your distressing dreams must not always involve a re-experiencing of the actual trauma. Some of your nightmares may have themes that are in some ways linked to the trauma. Others may seem completely different from the events which happened to you but may contain some of the feelings that you experienced during the trauma – such as your fear or helplessness.

c. Flashbacks

You may also experience flashbacks. **Flashbacks are less common than the repeated, distressing recollections of the trauma described earlier.** Flashbacks are sudden, vivid re-experiences of the trauma, which are accompanied by very strong emotions. They are so strong that you feel as if the trauma is really happening again and you can re-experience many of the bodily reactions that you felt at the time of the trauma. You can also lose awareness of the other things that are going on around you. You can even find yourself re-enacting some of the things that you did during the trauma. You may also have an acute awareness of sounds, smells, tastes and even bodily sensations like pain or discomfort, which feel like those that were present at the time of the trauma.

Flashbacks can last between a few seconds to several minutes (on rare occasions even hours) and sometimes you may even be unable to remember afterwards what happened to you during the flashback. You may feel ashamed about experiencing flashbacks and fear that you are losing complete control. You may feel reluctant to admit to anybody that you are experiencing flashbacks because you might fear that people think that you are 'mad'.

Flashbacks are not a sign that you are 'going mad' but signal that you are dealing with a very difficult and overwhelming experience, that your mind cannot make sense of yet.

NUMBING AND AVOIDANCE REACTIONS

Numbing and avoidance reactions are a way of controlling the strong emotions that you experience. This includes both the emotions that you may have experienced during the actual trauma itself and those that you feel now during the re-experiencing phases of the trauma.

Toni, who had survived a shipping disaster, described: *"For a long time after the trauma, I didn't feel anything. Other people commented on how strong and brave I was and I couldn't understand when a disaster counsellor asked me whether I wanted to talk through my experiences of the trauma. I couldn't feel anything about the trauma but also didn't want to think about it or be reminded of it. I just wanted to get on with my life as if nothing had happened. At times I felt hard and uncaring and wished that I could feel something."*

a. Numbing Reactions

Your system has the ability to protect itself from extreme emotional pain both during and after traumatic experiences. Trauma survivors frequently describe that they did not feel anything in response to what they later describe as emotionally very upsetting experiences. They often feel 'uncaring', because in order to survive they may have done things which would be unthinkable for them to do in their day to day life. You also may have experienced what felt like a complete shut-down of your emotions during some or all aspects of your trauma experience. Your trauma may have felt unreal like a dream to you at the time, almost as if it hadn't happened. This does not mean that you are a cold or uncaring person, rather it means that your survival system took over and numbed your reactions to help you survive the trauma.

Your feelings of emotional numbing can sometimes last for several days after the trauma. Others who were not directly involved in the trauma can often misunderstand these feelings as signs of strength and 'model' coping behaviour. You may have heard people say about you after the trauma that they were impressed at how strong you were and how well you coped with everything. Their comments may have given you the impression that you should cope with the trauma in this way and you may have felt ashamed as your feelings of numbness wore off and gave way to your real feelings about the trauma. You may have thought that you were not entitled to feel the emotional pain, the hurt, anger or upset or whatever other reactions you have had.

Your numbing responses may not always alternate with re-experiencing reactions. For some people the emotional numbing is there most of the time. If you feel that this describes you, you could find it difficult to feel any emotions at times. You might have difficulties at expressing love, intimacy and tenderness to those who had been close to you before the trauma. You may feel detached from those around you and find it harder to get on with people or to get emotionally close to someone. Others around you may have commented that you seem 'cold or uncaring', which may be exactly how you were feeling at the time, because you have difficulties now making a real connection to your underlying emotions.

It could help you and others to know that the emotional numbing has a kind of protective function. It is there because the emotions you experienced during the trauma were so very strong. Therefore, emotional numbing stops you from experiencing these very strong feelings but it can also stop you from enjoying the closeness which you may have had with people before the trauma. If you feel that this is a very big problem for you now, you will benefit from seeking help with this from a trained therapist (This guide will give you advice on how to do this).

b. Avoidance Reactions

You may find yourself not wanting to think or talk about your trauma. When someone asks you how you are feeling about it, you may try to change the topic, so that they won't ask you any further. This is a way of wanting to avoid the uncomfortable reactions that you may fear could be brought up if you talk or think about it.

Another form of avoidance are the so-called 'safety-behaviours'. You may find yourself still doing all or some of the things you used to do before the trauma, but you may be doing these differently now. For example, if you had a road traffic accident, you may still be driving, but now you drive much slower, check the mirrors all the time and brake far sooner. You do that to protect yourself because you want to avoid another accident from happening. However, in actual fact, you may be less safe now during your driving than you were before the accident. Other safety behaviour might be checking that things are alright all the time to make sure they are safe or having some special rituals, like looking out for certain things that you have told yourself would mean that you are safe or counting a certain number because you feel that this might protect you.

You may also have noticed that you are avoiding some or all situations that remind you of parts of your trauma. For example, if you have been in a road traffic accident you could be avoiding travelling in a car; if you have been assaulted, you may not leave your house at certain times; if you have been in a fire, you may avoid any form of open flame, like cooking on the flame of a gas cooker or lighting a candle; and so on.

Such avoidance is a very common response to trauma. The reason for your avoidance is that the situations which you avoid remind you so much of the trauma. They serve as a trigger for letting you experience the same strong fear responses that you associate with the trauma. **This means that every time you are confronted with a situation which reminds you of the trauma you will experience feelings similar to those you had during your trauma.** Because the intensity of these feelings makes you feel very uncomfortable, you avoid those triggers. Like the emotional numbing (described above), avoidance is another way of controlling your strong feelings about the trauma, because as long as you avoid the trigger situations you won't have to feel the emotional pain and physical discomfort associated with the trauma. While it may seem helpful to you not to have to feel these uncomfortable feelings, in the long run it is not helpful to avoid because this really limits your life, such as your ability to talk and think

31

freely and to go and do those things that you might have previously enjoyed.

REACTIONS OF INCREASED AROUSAL
(OR HYPER-AROUSAL)

The third group of reactions which you may be experiencing are reactions of increased arousal. These are closely linked to the bodily responses that you experienced during the trauma. These can occur during times when you are reminded of or re-experience part of the trauma. They can also happen in situations, which do not seem to be linked to aspects of the trauma at all.

Three weeks after his trauma, Toni started to experience very strong bodily reactions. He described: *"After my initial calm after the trauma, I started to feel really restless. I could no longer sleep at night, could not concentrate on anything and became angry with people for seemingly no reason. Sometimes, when I thought about aspects of the trauma, I felt so worked up that I got myself into a panic. During those times, I could feel the same fear that I had experienced during the trauma and my heart was beating so much that I felt as if I was going to have a heart attack and I felt all faint and dizzy."*

These responses are caused by adrenalin and other chemicals which are released through messages from your brain into your body's circulatory system. This is the same mechanism that would have happened during your trauma. During the trauma these chemicals were helpful for your survival because they enabled you to act in the way in which your survival system at the time thought it would be best for you. Now these arousal reactions may actually be interfering with your ability to lead a normal life. Although they are not dangerous, they are not helpful in situations where there is no danger and you don't really need the protection. **Some of the different reactions of increased arousal are briefly explained below:**

a. Difficulty falling or staying asleep

You may now have a problem with falling asleep or early morning waking. These episodes of sleeplessness can be, but do not have to be, related to bad dreams or nightmares. Sleeping can often also presents a particular problem for people whose trauma has happened while they were in their bed, asleep or lying down. Sleeping patterns may also be disrupted if you had to stay awake or alter your sleeping routines for prolonged periods during the trauma.

These responses are caused by an increase in adrenalin, which is your body's way of making you more alert in order to help you protect yourself from danger. This is, however, not very helpful in situations which are safe and in which you are trying to catch up on your sleep.

b. Irritability and/or outbursts of anger

Irritability and anger are very common reactions experienced by trauma survivors. Often there is no clear trigger for the irritability or the anger and you may find it difficult to be in control of yourself during these times. You may lash out and destroy things during these rages or you may just find yourself very irritable and bad tempered. You may find yourself picking arguments and you may also experience rage. This can happen seemingly out of the blue (in that case, most likely through a trigger that you so far have not been able to recognize) or if you feel that someone has triggered your threshold for patience, which is often much lower for people who are suffering from the effects of a trauma. You may also feel angry because you feel invaded by others when you just want to be left alone. Some people don't express their anger outwardly. They may feel it strongly inside them, but bottle it up and appear extremely calm to others on the surface.

Your anger is caused by a surge in your body's natural chemicals, such as adrenalin. This happens because your system got somehow triggered and now wants to protect you, because it feels that you may be in danger. It is therefore giving you the necessary chemicals that enable you to fight (either actual fighting, such as hurting somebody or taking it out on things, or verbally directed against others or inwardly against yourself). The problem, is that there is no threat and that you are unleashing your energy on an innocent person, often somebody who is close to and cares for you or you may be unfair and hurting to yourself. You may feel very guilty about your anger or irritability afterwards. **If anger is a problem for you, you may find it helpful to seek a therapist who can guide you in ways of coping with it.** There are also some brief guidelines in the later chapter on 'Coping with Anger and Irritability', which might help you with your anger.

c. Difficulties with concentration and memory

You may get easily distracted and find it difficult to concentrate on tasks. Your ability to read may be impaired as you can only concentrate on a few paragraphs in a book or magazine at a time. People may be talking to you and you find yourself drifting off only to notice when you come back to the conversation that you have lost the meaning of what they were trying to tell you. You may be far more forgetful than before the trauma. Your mind is still so pre-occupied with the trauma that there is little mental space left to concentrate on new information coming in from outside. **Your difficulties with concentration and memory are also linked to levels of increased arousal, caused by the adrenalin. In order to protect you from danger your mind is so alert that it is difficult for you to calm down and concentrate on things other than the trauma.**

d. Hyperalertness and exaggerated concern for your own and others' safety

Hyperalertness, also called Hypervigilance, describes what you experience when you are especially watchful of your environment and look out for potential danger, even when there is no obvious need to do so. When you are going out you may be especially careful about where you chose to sit, considering some seats as 'unsafe' areas, because you feel unprotected in those seating positions. You may also find yourself checking things, which were linked to the cause of trauma. You feel exaggerated concern for your own safety and you may be overprotective towards people who are close to you. You might worry about others if they haven't come home at the usual time. You might try and restrict the activity of those close to you, because you fear that otherwise something bad could happen to them.

All these reactions are caused by increased arousal and are part of your body's protective system. The trauma has made your mind so alert that it assesses what is going on in your environment all the time. This can be extremely draining for you as your senses are working overtime in order to achieve this high level of security. **Your whole system reacts as if you are still in acute danger.** It is almost as if it wants to make sure that if the trauma does happen again, this time you are going to be prepared. The problem, however, is that you don't really need this high level of security now, as the trauma has already happened and is unlikely to repeat itself. **As you come to terms and work through the trauma properly the intensity of these responses will gradually fade away.**

e. Exaggerated startle response

You may also have become very sensitive to noises and smells around you and you may find yourself more on edge and jumpy than you were before your trauma. Depending on the nature of your traumatic experience you may even get startled in response to a sudden, unexpected movement, such as when someone touches you from behind. When you experience these startle responses you feel 'out of control' and frightened because you feel you can't make sense of why you are reacting in this way. However, the startle reactions are yet another way of your system trying to protect you from danger. **Until you**

have worked through and recovered from your trauma your body will have difficulties with decreasing the intensity of your reactions, even though there is no real danger now.

f. Bodily reactions in response to situations that remind you of your trauma

The bodily reactions you experience in response to the situations which remind you of your trauma differ between different individuals. You may suffer from increased heart beats, may find yourself over-breathing, may feel physically sick or be suffering from diarrhoea. You may sweat intensely or feel very cold and shiver. You may even experience pain or discomfort in some parts of your body, which were injured or hurt during the trauma. Although these parts may now have physically healed, part of your body still remembers and can make you feel the pain again. These are called body memories. While distressing to you, all these reactions are part of your body's danger warning system, which does a too thorough job and therefore gets in the way of you leading a normal life.

1.7 Other reactions to trauma

REACTIONS LINKED TO LOSS OF A PERSON CLOSE TO YOU

If you have lost a person close to you during a trauma you will not have had any time to prepare yourself for their death. Their death will have come as a sudden shock to you. Moreover, their death may have been very untimely. It is harder to come to terms with the death of a young person, and it will be especially difficult for you to heal if it is your own child whom you have lost through death.

Grieving is such a painful process that you may wish to avoid it at all costs. However, blocking out the experience of your loss for a long time will not be helpful to you. It may lead to even further complications in your life. Unresolved grieving has been linked to a number of psychological problems, for example, anxiety and panic problems, depression, eating problems and physical problems, such as, heart disease, lowered resistance to infections, allergies, and others. Therefore, it would be important for you to learn to allow yourself to face your grief.

This booklet is not comprehensive enough to outline the process of grieving in further detail but some books for further reading are listed in the reference section at the back. It would also be advisable for you to seek help from a skilled trauma counsellor or a therapist, who can support you in working through your loss.

PHYSICAL DISFIGUREMENT/LOSS OF PARTS OF YOUR BODY

The loss of parts of your body, such as limbs, or the loss of your former looks through physical disfigurement can be just as painful as losing another person through death. **A part of your old Self has died through these losses.** It will take time for you to adjust and get used to your new Self. **In order for you to heal it is important that you allow yourself to process your feelings of grief, bitterness and sadness.**

CHRONIC PAIN

You may also experience chronic pain problems, for which you may have made repeated visits to your doctor and other medical professionals, but they can't find anything wrong. Your injuries may have healed but you still feel the pain. This doesn't mean that your pain isn't real. Sometimes, this type of **pain can be part of your body's memories of the trauma.** If this is the case, you may find that if you are thinking about or are being reminded of the trauma your pain gets worse. Sometimes this pain can shift and resolve as a result of you processing the trauma. In order to achieve this, **you would probably need the help of a skilled trauma therapist, who would know how to work in ways that would help you process your bodily symptoms.** Sometimes, however, this is not possible, may be because the pain is there for some other reasons. Often if this is the case, it may be useful for you to also attend a pain management programme, which is aimed at helping you find ways of coping with the chronic pain in ways that least interfere with your ability to lead a normal life. Your doctor should be able to recommend a pain management clinic near you.

SEXUAL DIFFICULTIES

Both your high level of tension and your difficulties with tolerating closeness to others at this time can impair your enjoyment of sex. Your sexual relationship may suffer as a result and may not feel the same as before the trauma. The trauma took you by surprise in a way that you did not expect and you temporarily felt out of control. **In order to enjoy sexual closeness with your partner you need to able to relax and let go of some of your control.** However, because you are still coming to terms with the trauma you may feel tense and pre-occupied much of the time and will find it very difficult to relax enough to let go of some of your control. For men this may mean that they have difficulties in achieving or holding an erection. Woman may not be able to tolerate penetration and both men and women may not be able to reach orgasm.

Sexual difficulties are especially common after a trauma which involved violence of a physical or sexual nature. Your sexual difficulties may also be linked to physical disfigurement or loss of parts of your body, which resulted from the trauma. **You will often need to allow yourself time to come to terms with these losses and the resulting changes in your sexual lifestyle and their impact on your relationship.**

When you have enjoyed a good sexual relationship before the trauma your partner may find it difficult to understand why this should have changed. **Your partner may blame you or feel that this change is his or her fault.** This could be a very upsetting experience to you because you may feel that although you still love your partner you are unable to reach physical and/or emotional closeness and are letting your partner down.

DEPRESSION

The experience of depression is common after trauma. You may find yourself crying easily and you may feel hopeless, low in energy and without interest in doing anything that you would normally enjoy. You may also have lost your appetite. **If you feel that you are at serious risk of harming yourself, you should get in touch with your doctor and ask for help immediately.**

If your depression is linked to the trauma, it is likely that it will lift as you work through and heal from your trauma. **Sometimes, however, if your depression is very severe and stops you from working through your trauma, you could find it helpful to take some medication.** This can be prescribed to you by your doctor or a psychiatrist. **Two books that can help you to understand more about depression are also listed in the reference section at the back.**

GUILT/SELF-BLAME

a. Blaming yourself for all or parts of the trauma and/or your actions during it

Often, especially when the loss of other persons occurred during the trauma, people blame themselves for all or some parts of the trauma or their responses and actions during the trauma. It is very common for people to go through the trauma again and again looking out for things they feel they should have done differently to prevent what happened.

Part of working through the trauma will involve you learning to accept the way in which you behaved during the trauma. It may be helpful to remind yourself that at the time of the trauma you had no time to think things through and your survival system took over. You might have behaved differently under normal, more controllable conditions. Given the circumstances of the trauma, your reactions were normal even though they may seem strange to you now. **You tried to cope as well as you could given the very difficult circumstances of the trauma.**

b. Feeling that it should have been you who died instead of the other person

You may have been in a trauma where another person died. **You may feel guilty about being alive while the other person or people died.** When this happens surviving often seems harder than dying. Surviving means living with the knowledge that another person lost their life and it may feel as if you don't have a right to live. Your feelings of guilt may be so strong that, although not actually dead, you may live your life in a way that deprives you of all the pleasures that make life enjoyable and worth living. **This prevents you from moving on and healing from the trauma.** Of course, things have not been fair. Nobody should have died in the trauma.

By living your life in the way that you do because of your guilt it is as if neither of you is alive. This may be your attempt to gain control over the uncontrollable. It is as if you feel that by living your life as if you were also dead, you may be able to bring back to life the person or people who really died. However, this can never happen even though your wish for this to happen is very understandable. **Recovering from trauma will require you to accept that none of your actions can now be undone, and that you are punishing yourself unnecessarily for something that you cannot change.** The realization that you cannot change things and that you have to learn to accept them, can be extremely painful. **However, before healing can begin it is important for you to allow yourself to feel and work through this pain, so that eventually you can start to re-build your own life despite your experience of the trauma.**

1.8 What is Post-Traumatic Stress Disorder (PTSD)?

You may have been told by your doctorr, by a psychiatrist, a clinical psychologist or another mental health care professional that you are suffering from **Post-Traumatic Stress Disorder.**

Post-Traumatic Stress Disorder, or PTSD for short, is a name which is given to a particular range and combination of reactions after a trauma. It is a framework which helps health care professionals understand which reactions you may be experiencing and how to best help you. After a trauma most people experience some or most of the reactions that are described in this booklet. However, **if you experience those reactions for longer than one month,** your reactions may be given the name **Post-Traumatic Stress Disorder** (PTSD). Depending on how many reactions and the type and severity of the reactions that you are experiencing you could have **partial or full-blown Post-Traumatic Stress Disorder.**

If you have been told that you have Post-Traumatic Stress Disorder this means that you have the same reactions as those experienced by almost every person after a trauma, but that **your reactions have lasted longer than a month** and **may be at a more severe level.** Some people do not even experience any reactions at all immediately after the trauma and **it is only several months later that post-trauma reactions occur.** Once they occur they may be quite severe and often last longer than a month.

You may feel (and some health care professionals may seem to believe this) that because you have been diagnosed as suffering from Post-Traumatic Stress Disorder that you may be 'deficient' or 'sick' or 'mentally abnormal'. **As explained in this booklet you are experiencing reactions which are natural and very understandable reactions** given the very sudden and distressing experiences that you have been through because of your trauma. **You are not abnormal but what you experienced at the time of the trauma was sudden and unexpected** and it now makes you react in these ways because you haven't completely worked through and come to terms with what happened during your experience and may be also afterwards.

If you have, or suspect that you may have, Post-Traumatic Stress Disorder you may find it beneficial to seek help from a clinical psychologist, a specialist trauma counsellor or other trauma therapist who will be able to support and guide you through your recovery process. It will be important for you to find a Health Care Professional who is able to understand what you are going through at the moment and who does not label you as abnormal. Many people who have post trauma reactions and even PTSD recover naturally. However, when you have had these reactions for **eight months or longer** and they are still disrupting your ability to lead a normal life, it would be important for you to ask your doctor to put you in touch with a specialist trauma therapist or trauma counsellor for an assessment. Sometimes, if you are part of a legal compensation claim your solicitor can also arrange this for you.

As a general rule, the sooner you start working through your trauma the quicker you can move toward recovery. In the back of this guide you will find an outline of professionals who may be able to help you.

1.9 Why don't all people react in the same ways to trauma?

You may wonder why some people get Post-Traumatic Stress Disorder and others do not. You may ask yourself, why your reactions seem stronger and more severe than your friend's reactions, although your friend experienced exactly the same trauma as you. This is because every person's experience of life and therefore of the events that make up their life is different.

Because of the differences between people and their experiences of themselves, and their environment, each person's response to a trauma is different. Trauma affects people in different ways, because each person can only experience a trauma through their own feelings and observations at the time. Because we are all individuals, our experiences can differ. Even though people may have different experiences and reactions to the same trauma, **all experiences and reactions are equally valid. It is important to remember that there is no right or wrong way of responding to a trauma.** It is therefore very important that you **don't allow others or yourself to undermine or invalidate your experiences and reactions. Equally, it is important that you respect other people's experiences and reactions in the same way that yours deserve to be respected by others.**

Although, there may also be similarities in the way in which people experience and respond to the same trauma, these can vary in their severity, the time when they first started and the length of time during which they are present. On reading this guide, you may find that you experienced some reactions that are described, but not others. This is normal as not everybody experiences all the reactions described. However, if you do experience all the reactions described this means that the traumatic experience has been especially overwhelming and disturbing to you. **Remember that this is not your fault and that there are steps that you can now take to recover from the effect of the trauma.**

Part 2

coping with the trauma

Part 2

2.1 The process of re-building your life

As much as you would like your reactions to go away quickly, this may not happen. **You need to recognize that the process of recovery may take time and is unique to each person.**

Here is an example of Gina's recovery from her trauma:

Gina, a cashier who recovered successfully from an armed robbery at the bank where she worked, described her process of recovery in the following way: "At first it felt as if my world had shattered into a thousand pieces. Nothing seemed to make sense any longer. Even the simplest things felt impossible for me to do. It was as if I had unlearned and forgotten everything that I had once known. It seemed that all of the old me had gone. I felt as if I was faced with having to do a puzzle where none of the pieces fitted together or made sense. Slowly, however, by working through the trauma with my therapist, some of the pieces started to fit into place. Initially only a few pieces seemed to fit, while the rest were still lying scattered around. However, with time the puzzle grew and the faster it grew the more I could start to see of the overall picture. There were setbacks too. For example, when sections of the puzzle, which I had built up in isolation, just didn't seem to fit into the larger picture. During those times I often felt like giving up. It had taken me so much effort to build that section and now all that seemed wasted. I felt so drained and tired. I was also frightened not knowing what the finished puzzle would look like.

However I did persevere and was slowly able to recover from my trauma. I learned to recognize that the puzzle will never be finished, that the building of it is an ongoing process. This process will continue throughout my life and the picture of the puzzle will never stay exactly the same. However, by the time I finished my therapy, I had worked on enough parts of the puzzle to feel that I had re-gained control over many aspects of my life again. While I will never forget the trauma, it has now become part of my overall picture of life. It has become a part of the puzzle. This means that the trauma now no longer takes over and controls my life. I am able to look forward to the future again and it feels to me that the experience of working through my trauma has helped me to become a more understanding and tolerant person. It took me over a year to reach this stage of recovery."

There are no clear guidelines about how long it takes to recover from trauma. Like Gina you may experience times when you feel stuck or even find yourself 'going backwards' rather than moving on. Whatever your stage in the recovery process, Gina's story illustrates that recovery from trauma takes time and can be a long and painful process. None of us like to experience pain, whether physical or emotional, but in order to recover from trauma it is helpful and healing to experience your pain and distress. The aim of recovery is not to get stuck in that pain but to work through it and process it in a way, which releases it so that it can then leave your whole system and you feel free from it. Your picture of life will never be the same as before the trauma. Your trauma will become a part of that picture but will no longer feel as if it controls all of your life.

Many people who have successfully recovered from their trauma feel that they have grown a lot and that their life now has qualities, which it did not seem to have before the trauma. All this may seem surprising to you at this stage in your process of recovery and it is therefore very important that you persevere despite some feelings of hopelessness and despair that you may be holding inside yourself.

2.2 Some things that might help you start with your process of recovery

As the reactions to trauma and recovery from it are diverse it will not be possible to cover the wide range of methods that people may find helpful for their recovery in much detail within the scope of this booklet. **However, some things that other trauma survivors have found helpful and that may help you to start with the first steps in your process of recovery are outlined below.**

GETTING IT OUT – WORKING IT THROUGH!

As described before, your reactions to the trauma may feel very strong and overwhelming to you. Your natural response may be to try not to think or talk about what has happened. When people ask you about the trauma, your answers may be vague and only touch briefly on the event. This could be because you feel uncomfortable talking in more detail about what happened or because you feel others couldn't handle hearing what you have been through. Others around you may shy away from asking you altogether, perhaps because they do not know how to ask you or may be frightened of upsetting you. Sometimes, people feel that they have talked to others about their trauma, when they really have only outlined very few aspects of what really happened to them. When people start their therapy they often discover that they have not really had the opportunity to talk their trauma through in detail with others around them.

Your difficulties talking about your trauma and other people's difficulties asking you and hearing about it are all entirely common and understandable reactions. **However, in order to help you heal from the trauma, it needs to be told. What is more, it needs to be done in every little detail.** This is contrary to the beliefs that many people around you and even you yourself may have. You and others may feel: 'it is better if it is left alone' or 'it will go away if it isn't thought or talked about'. However, this will not usually happen. The trauma and the feelings you link to it will not usually just disappear. **In order to come to terms with the trauma, you must give yourself the opportunity to talk it through.**

It may even be that you want to talk about your trauma or have tried to, but you can't find words for it or can't put it into any cohesive language at all. This could be due to the way in which your brain functioned during the trauma. Recent research[1] has shown that it is entirely possible, during a traumatic event for parts of our brain to shut down temporarily. Sometimes, when our system is completely concerned with our own survival, it will put all its energy into those brain parts that need to stay functioning during the trauma. To be able to do that it seems to shut down those parts that are not so important for the immediate survival. The part that shuts down is called the hippocampus and its task is to organize information, make sense of things to help put them into a meaningful language.

If this has happened, then after a trauma it might be difficult to put the experience into proper language and talk about it. If this is the case for you, you do not need to worry because there are different ways in which you can recover from a trauma than only through talking about it. Recovery for you needs to involve working through your trauma by imagining it in a way that you can relive it in every detail and with all its sensations so that these can be processed and you can be freed of them. **This is not dangerous, but, it is best done in therapy and a skilled trauma therapist will know how to help you with this.**

[1Nadel, L. & Jacobs, W.J. (1996) – The role of the hippocampus in PTSD, panic and phobia. In N. Kato (Ed.), Hippocampus: Functions and clinical relevance (pp. 455-463). Elsevier: Amsterdam]

WAYS OF TALKING THROUGH THE TRAUMA

Talking through the trauma will not be easy for you because in the process you are likely to experience very strong emotions (these are part of your re-experiencing reactions). **If you are worried that your feelings when you talk about your trauma may be so strong that you can't control them, you should contact your family doctor who can arrange for professional help from a trauma counsellor, clinical psychologist or other skilled mental health care worker.** They will be able to advise you whether it is indeed the right time to talk through your trauma. Sometimes it is better to wait until you have more energy and support in your life before you start this kind of talking-through work.

However, **if you feel fairly confident that it is the right time to talk through your trauma,** even if this may bring up emotions and bodily sensations in you, then **you could try one or several of the following:**

1. If you have a very supportive partner or friend, who you feel could cope with hearing, you may like to tell your story.

2. Alternatively, you may find it easier to write your story down on paper rather than describing it aloud to somebody. You may like to share this with your partner or a person who is close to you and/or your therapist.

3. Another option which people often find helpful is to talk your story into a tape or videotape recorder. You may want to add bits and listen to it several times after you have recorded it.Don't forget to include your emotional reactions.

4. If all of these seem too difficult for you at this stage you may want to try painting or drawing some of the aspects of your trauma first. You do not have to be a particularly good artist to do this because you really want to just try and express what it felt like for you during the trauma.

However, if you do any of these, remember you must always stop if you feel that your feelings or emotions are getting too strong for you to control. If this happens and you are talking to another person, please let them know what is happening and arrange to take a break. It is usually more helpful to leave the room and switch to a completely different activity, such as taking a walk outside or finding something to do in the house that distracts you. If you are writing your story down, are audio/video-recording it or painting/drawing it – do the same, take a break and do something to distract yourself.

If these strong reactions continue to be overwhelming, please seek advice from a health care professional, such as your doctor or your therapist.

TACKLING AVOIDANCE

As outlined before, it is understandable that after a trauma you may try to avoid various activities or situations that remind you of the trauma. In some circumstances, for example if there is a continued risk to your safety, it may obviously be most helpful to you to avoid that activity or situation. However, **in most instances the activities or** situations that you connect to the trauma will now no longer be dangerous to you. In order to heal from your trauma and for your trauma not to control the way in which you lead your life, **you will gradually need to learn to confront these avoided activities and situations again.**

A good way of doing this is to confront the avoided activity or situation in a gradual and stepwise way. If there are some activities or situations which you feel ready to confront, here is what you might like to do:

> **a. Break the activity or situation down into small parts that are connected to it and order these as practise steps from easiest to hardest.**

For example, Sue who was described at the beginning of this booklet first started to tackle her subsequent avoidance of driving in a car after her Road Traffic Accident, by breaking her activity of driving down and ordering her practise steps in the following way:

1. Open door of car and sit in it.
2. Turn the key to start the car and sit in it.
3. Put the car into gear and drive a few yards down the street and back again.
4. Drive down the whole of the street and back.
5. Drive round the neighbourhood and back.
6. Go for a five minute drive in the car.
7. Drive down an A road to the nearest big town
and so on...

b. Start practising the easiest step of the activity first and only go on to the next step when you feel comfortable with the practise step before.

c. You can give yourself a rating for your level of comfort, between 0 –10 (where 0 is very comfortable, and 10 is the worst discomfort you have felt) on a step each time you practise it. You should find that with repeated practise your levels of discomfort on that step will drop. When they are down to a rating of 1-2, you may start working on the next step.

Sue, for example, practised every day to open her car and sit in it and it took her about three weeks before she felt comfortable doing this. She was able to give herself a comfort rating of 2, before she decided to move to the next step. Only then did she move on to the next practise step of turning the key to start the car and sit in it.

When you start your practise activities, you may initially feel very anxious. **Remember, you feel anxious because a part of your mind still believes that the activity or situation that you have avoided and are now practising is dangerous.** Your body is therefore giving out signals which make you feel as if you are in danger, even when you are not. **Through practise you can teach your body that the activity or situation is now no longer dangerous.**

When you practise it is therefore common to feel some anxiety. However, if this anxiety feels completely overwhelming to you, stop and go back to an easier practise step in your ladder of activities. You may also find the breathing exercises, below, helpful. **If your anxiety continues to feel extremely overwhelming and persists you should discuss this with your doctor or therapist.**

COPING WITH SAFETY BEHAVIOURS

'You may not be avoiding activities that remind you of the trauma altogether, but you may have a range of safety behaviours that you use in order to protect yourself from what now feels like a dangerous situation. For example, when you are travelling as a passenger in a car after a road traffic accident, you may now be using an 'imaginary brake' or 'scan the road ahead really intensely and shout out when you see cars pulling out' or you may even tell the driver how to drive. As explained before, these safety behaviours usually don't make you any safer. On the contrary, they make you or others overcautious and therefore can make you less safe. Also, your repeated use of safety behaviours prevents you from learning that the situation has not actually become more dangerous since your trauma. Therefore if you observe yourself using safety behaviours it is important for you to find ways in which you can drop them.

a. One method is to write down a list of all the safety behaviours you are aware of. Then for each one, plan what you might try to do instead of using it. For example, you might decide that rather than using the 'imaginary brake' – you will immediately relax your feet and gently move your toes about whenever you feel the urge to protect yourself. Or rather than clutching your hands round your seat as safety behaviour, you will hold them together and gently and rub them.

b. Another strategy is to distract yourself from using the safety behaviour by focussing on other interesting things around you. Try and explain to yourself why you might be using safety behaviours and why they are not really very helpful to you or others around you.

COPING WITH ANXIETY

There may be times when you feel completely overwhelmed by your anxiety. **Your anxiety is a natural response and part of the increased arousal responses,** which were described earlier. Although it can feel very uncomfortable, **the anxiety in itself is not harmful to you.** During times of anxiety, you may experience feelings of panic and tension. Often this is accompanied by an increased rate in your breathing. This is sometimes called hyperventilation.

When you feel this way, your automatic response will often be to breathe even faster because it feels to you as if you are not getting enough oxygen. However, the faster you breathe and the more oxygen you get the more dizzy and faint you will feel. Also, because you haven't taken the time to breathe deeply, the oxygen won't distribute evenly to all those parts in your body that need it. Therefore rather than feeling calmer, you often feel even more agitated if you breathe in that way.

It is rather like flooding a car with petrol by pressing too hard on the accelerator. Although the car needs the petrol to drive, if it gets too much it can't drive at all. When you get too much oxygen this will make you feel less rather than more in control. **It is therefore important that you start to breathe slowly and gently rather than fast and shallow.**

You might like to try the following:

Although it may feel difficult at first, **allow yourself to become aware of your breathing.**

- Notice the temperature of your breath and stay with this a little while.
- Notice the pace of your breathing and how fast it is. Allow yourself to gently slow it down. Notice the difference to how it feels when you take gentle slow breaths.
- Then notice the depth of your breathing. Notice how shallow your breathing is. Put one hand on your stomach and allow yourself to take in gentle and deep breaths. Notice that as you breathe in your hand on your stomach goes up and as you breathe out your hand goes down. Just follow that gentle, deep rhythm of breathing and notice how comfortable it is.
- Even imagine a colour that for you would now feel healing and imagine your breath becoming that soothing and healing colour. Allow yourself to take in as much of that healing as you can.
- When you are finished just very gently stop and remind yourself that you can experience the soothing rhythm of your breath any time you want.

You may even speak this breathing exercise onto a tape, CD or minidisk. You can then listen to it or use it as often as you like.

When you first start to try to relax your breathing, you may find it a very difficult thing to do. It will be especially difficult if you try it during times when your anxiety is high. **It is therefore more helpful to you if you can start practising to slow down your breathing during times when you are not so anxious.**

When you first start practising it is also helpful to do this in a place where you are **private** and **will not be disturbed.** Later when you have mastered using the breathing exercises effectively, you should be able to apply them in any situation. Like most people, **you will probably find that you will have to practise these breathing exercises regularly before they can be of help to you during times of real anxiety.**

There are many other ways of coping with anxiety, such as relaxation programmes or distraction techniques and it is not within the scope of this booklet to address these. Certain classes, like Yoga, Tai Chi, Meditation or Mindfulness can also help you learn to control your breathing and your body differently so that you feel less anxious. May be you would like to join one of these. However, **if you are concerned about your anxiety or panic responses, please consult your doctor ask him for places where you might get further help, such as seeing a therapist.**

COPING WITH ANGER OR IRRITABILITY

Like anxiety, anger or irritability is also linked to your reactions of increased arousal. **During these times of anger you have an increased amount of energy, which you can use in destructive or constructive ways.** While you are experiencing anger you may find it difficult to stay rational and you may say or do things which you may later regret and feel ashamed about.

It may therefore be helpful to remove yourself altogether from the situation, in which you started to feel angry. If you often get angry in the presence of your partner you may like to have an agreement with him/her beforehand that you will need some space and want to be left alone when you feel your anger building up. It might also be helpful to explain to your partner that it doesn't mean that you don't love him/her or care when you walk out, but that you need the space in order to let off steam, away from those people whom it might hurt.

You could use up the increase in your energy by going for a vigorous run or by applying yourself to a physical task, which does not cause hurt to yourself or others. Often, simply getting out of the situation, in which you started to feel your anger increase can be helpful.

If you have continuous urges to hurt yourself or others around you or find that you are not doing very well at controlling your anger, you would probably benefit from talking to your doctor and you may consider finding a skilled trauma therapist who can help you with controlling your anger more constructively.

SLEEPING PROBLEMS

As you are starting to recover from your trauma you will often find that your sleeping problems also improve.

The following might help you with your sleeping problems:

- Stop drinking coffee, tea, chocolate drinks or alcohol too close to bedtime.
- Do not take any naps or extra sleep during the day, even if you are tired from your sleeping difficulties the night before.
- Stick to a regular night time routine, i.e. go to bed at around the same time each night.
- Do not deal with problems last thing at night.
- Sometimes relaxation exercises, a soothing bath or physical exercise to tire you out, before your bedtime can help.
- If you can't get yourself to sleep within 30 minutes of going to bed, get up and do another activity, such as reading a magazine or watching TV. After 15 minutes go back to bed again and try to get yourself to sleep. If you still can't fall asleep this time, get up again and do another activity. Repeat this process as long as necessary and only use your bed for sleeping in.
- Keep a record of how much sleep you get each night. This may give you some clues about particular patterns in your sleeping such as, for example, sleeping particularly badly after you had a very inactive day. You may also find it helpful to record your dreams.
- You may also consider using alternative, natural remedies

to help you with your sleeping problems. You may like to consult a good healthfood store, a homeopath or different, qualified herbal practitioner to find out whether there is something that might help you naturally. Aromatherapy oils can also be very supportive in helping you to relax. You might like to use a burner with some soothing oils at night. To know which ones are right for you to use, you may like to consult a qualified aromatherapist. Also certain Bach Flower remedies might be helpful in supporting your sleep. For this it would be advisable to consult with a trained Bach Flower Practitioner. A list of how you might find qualified, alternative practitioners is provided in the back of this guide.

If your sleeping problems persist and cause you considerable discomfort, you may benefit from discussing your particular sleeping difficulties with your doctor and also your therapist, if you have one.

SEXUAL DIFFICULTIES

This book is not comprehensive enough to address possible solutions to your sexual difficulties in detail. However, if your problems seem to be linked to your high levels of tension you may like to consider the following:

- If you have a supportive partner explain that your sexual difficulties at the moment are linked to your strong reactions to the trauma. Your reactions are so strong because you are still trying to come to terms with what happened to you. Explain that because of this it can be difficult for you to relax enough to become sexually aroused. This does not mean, however, that you don't love or care for your partner any longer.

- You could try to get sexually close to your partner through other forms of sexual contact rather than having intercourse. You could stroke and caress each other or give each other a massage, for example.

- Take time to be together when you are feeling in a more relaxed mood. For example, listening to some relaxing music, trying breathing exercises or having your room filled by your favourite scent may help you to feel more relaxed.

- Remove those things around you that could remind you of the trauma and trigger distressing memories for you.

- Try and create stimulating images in your mind that are totally unrelated to the trauma. These may help to distract you enough to be able to let go of some of your control and become sexually aroused. If your distressing memories keep interfering try and re-focus on the stimulating images again. Be prepared to give this time and persevere if you are not initially successful.

There are several books that you may find helpful in exploring alternative ways of sexual intimacy. Two books are listed in the 'Further Reading' section at the back of this booklet.

If your sexual difficulties continue you should discuss these with your doctor or your therapist. This could be especially helpful to you if your trauma was one where violence of a physical or sexual nature occurred or if you suffered physical disfigurement or a loss of parts of your body and your sexual difficulties are related to this.

ALCOHOL AND DRUGS

Sometimes people use alcohol or drugs, such as cannabis, in order to cope with their distressing reactions in response to trauma. As the emotional pain caused by the reactions to trauma can be very overwhelming, alcohol or drugs often seem an easy way to gain some temporary relief from the pain.

The problem with using alcohol or drugs to cope with the pain, however, is that although you might get some temporary relief, they stop you from successfully working through the trauma. In order to process the trauma and recover from it you will have to allow yourself to face some of the emotional discomfort and learn different ways of coping with it.

If alcohol and/or drug use is a problem for you it might be helpful for you to talk to your doctor, who should be able to put you in touch with someone who can help. If you have one, you should also let your therapist know about this, as

excessive use of alcohol or drugs can make it very difficult for you to succeed in therapy.

MEDICATION

In order to recover from your trauma, you will have to deal with the trauma and work through it. As outlined above, **this often involves confronting some very uncomfortable and painful emotions.** Most of the time you will be able to cope with these without the use of medication.

Sometimes, however, it can be helpful to take some medication while working through your trauma in therapy. Medication may be especially helpful during those times when you may be too depressed as a result of the trauma to be able to work effectively in your therapy. During those times anti-depressant medication could be a helpful addition to therapy. Medication on a temporary basis may also be helpful if your sleeping problems are so severe that they prevent you from getting any rest at all.

Sometimes, if your trauma reactions seem unmanageably strong, medication can be helpful while you are on a waiting-list for therapy.

Medication may also be helpful when there are so many other stresses in your life, that they prevent you from being able to work through the trauma at this stage. However, most of the time you will be able to work through your psychological reactions to the trauma without the need for medication.

If you do consider taking medication, it is important that you see a properly qualified medical professional, such as a psychiatrist, who should have had some experience of working with survivors of trauma. Your doctor may also be able to help, although he/she may prefer to refer you to a psychiatrist.

Another option might also be for you to explore trying some herbal remedies that could support you while you are working through your trauma. Remedies that people have found helpful, include Homeopathic Remedies, Bach Flower Remedies and taking extra herbal or nutritional supplements, such as specific Vitamins or Minerals. In order to find those remedies that would be helpful to you and to use these correctly, you should consult with a qualified practitioner in the area, which you would like to try out. At the back of this booklet there is a list of holistic organizations, which keep a register of their qualified practitioners.

2.3 How to get Professional Help

Not everybody needs professional help to recover from their trauma. However, in order to recover from a trauma everybody has to come to terms with it in such a way that it is integrated into their experience of life. Whether you might benefit from therapy depends, among others factors, on:

- the type and severity of your particular trauma
- the type and severity of your psychological reactions to the trauma
- the nature of your previous life experiences
- your style of coping
- the support network surrounding you

Most types of trauma can be helped by therapy, even if it has been very severe. Many people say that therapy has been a very helpful experience for them. People often feel that experiencing a trauma is so different to anything else that they have ever experienced or known before and therefore it has a huge impact on their lives. Part of therapy therefore often involves taking stock of and re-evaluating one's Self and life. Many people have found that therapy not only enabled them to work through and heal from the adverse effects of their trauma, but also helped them to find a different direction and more meaningful purpose and in life.

There are many types of therapy available and it can be very confusing to decide on what might benefit you most. Whatever therapy you chose, it is important that it will involve some deeper level processing of the trauma rather than just talking about it in a more superficial way, or may be not touching on it at all. Non-specialist counselling has been shown not to help the effects of trauma. It is important that the type of therapy you choose can help you to experience your feelings, your bodily symptoms and your thoughts in connection with the traumatic event.

Research shows that **Cognitive Behavioural Psychotherapy (CBT)** or **Cognitive Therapy (CT)** or **Behaviour Therapy (BT)**, which use similar approaches to the ones outlined in this booklet seems to be quite effective in helping people who suffer from trauma. These forms of therapy work in a very collaborative way with people and involve both some form of processing and working through the trauma, as well as some work on helping a person re-claim their life as best as they can.

Another technique that is often used in combination with CBT or CT, but sometimes also with other types of therapies, is **EMDR.** This stands for **Eye Movement Desensitization and Reprocessing.** It is a technique that was especially developed for trauma and it can be very effective also in helping to work through trauma when a person finds it difficult to put their experience into words and is struggling to make any cohesive sense of it. It is also a very helpful technique for people who suffer from a lot of body memories as a result of their trauma. EMDR involves feeling and processing the experiences of the trauma on a deeper level, involving feelings, bodily symptoms and thoughts. The therapist will induce some form of movement, which often travels from one side of the body to the other side (bilateral). This can be done either through you tracking the movement of your therapist's hand with your eyes, or it can be done through your therapist gently tapping or pressing your hands in alternation or through you listening to a special type of music, which moves from side to side. During these movements you work through the trauma in a special way. EMDR can sometimes work very rapidly and it can heal on a deep level. If you would like to read more on how this particular technique works some resources for this are listed in the 'Further Reading' section at the back of this booklet.

There are also some new trauma therapies, the so-called energy therapies, such as **Thought Field Therapy**, which some people have found effective in helping them heal from their trauma. As yet there has not been much research done on the effectiveness of the therapeutic techniques that these therapies use. Many of them seem to incorporate principles that have been used in Eastern medicine, such as working with the body's meridians. If you are considering trying **Hypnotherapy**, it is important that you chose a practitioner, who also has specialist experience of working with people who have been traumatized, because for some types of trauma, hypnotherapy has been shown not to be helpful.

Much of the trauma is experienced in the body and therefore other forms of bodywork or body therapy can also **be very helpfully used in conjunction with specialist psychological trauma therapy.** You might want to consider, for example, Acupuncture, Aromatherapy Massage, Deep Tissue Massage,

Shiatsu, Reflexology or Cranio-sacral Therapy. Learning Yoga, Meditation and Mindfulness Techniques could also be a very helpful additional support during you trauma therapy. However, it is important to ensure that you do this work with a person who is properly trained and qualified.

Whatever, therapy you decide to use, it is important that you feel comfortable and safe with your therapist, that you know they are properly qualified and they have experience of working with trauma. You may even find it helpful to use some of the suggestions made in this guide with your therapist during your recovery work.

If, after reading this, you feel that you would like to get some professional help, below are some suggestions on how you might go about this.

If you feel that you may need professional help, please do not see this as a sign of personal weakness. Recognising that you are not able to move forward on your own is often a sign of great personal strength.

A good starting point is to find out whether your doctor might be able to recommend a therapist who could help you. Most doctors know of therapists, such as **Clinical Psychologists, Psychiatrists, Clinical Nurse Specialists, Community Psychiatric Nurses (CPNs)** or others, who might be able to help you with your problems. It is important that you are referred to a therapist who has been properly trained and who has experience in the area of trauma psychology. If your doctor doesn't seem very understanding or doesn't know how to get you some help, than it might be helpful for you to ask for a second opinion from a different doctor.

At the moment, many Mental Health Care Professionals working within the National Health Service operate long waiting lists for therapy. This could mean that you will be assessed but then experience a waiting time before you can be seen for therapy. **If this guide has been given to you by your therapist after your assessment, it might help you during your waiting time, until you can start working through your trauma in greater depth during your therapy.**

If you feel that a long waiting time before you can start with your therapy would be very difficult for you, you should discuss this with your doctor and also the therapist who assessed you.. There may be a priority service or they may be able to suggest some other compromise, such as taking medication for a little while or for you to be able to get in touch with your therapist during your waiting time, when things seem intolerably difficult for you.

Alternatively, if you can afford to pay, you may want to consider a referral to a private therapist or trauma treatment service. If you do this, however, it is important that you ensure that your therapist is properly qualified, receives regular supervision and has experience in the area of trauma psychology. It could be very helpful for you to contact the professional body or therapeutic parent organization for the special therapy you are interested in. The contact organizations differ from country to country, but the most relevant for the United Kingdom and the Republic of Ireland are listed under the 'Contact Addresses' section at the back of this guide. Contact addresses for all the other English speaking countries can be obtained from The Oxford Stress and Trauma Centre and details on how to do this are at the back. Most of these will keep a register of their qualified therapists or will be able to tell you how to get one.

2.4 If you are in therapy, stay with it – don't give up too soon!

At times working through a trauma in therapy can be difficult. As Gina described in the account of her recovery from trauma, there were times when she felt that she was going backwards rather than forwards. This is not unusual during therapy and when you are in such a phase, you may be tempted to throw it all in and give up. Please don't! Try to stay with it and talk your difficulties through with your therapist. There could be good reasons why you feel you are not progressing at that stage.

In order for you to be helped in therapy it is important that you discuss your feelings openly and honestly with your therapist. This includes discussing those times when therapy is difficult for you. If you have found an experienced and qualified trauma therapist, he/she will understand when you feel that way and will be able to explore the reasons for this with you. Together, the two of you can work out ways in which those times could be made easier for you. If you feel that your therapist doesn't seem to understand, despite you trying to talk things through with them; or if you feel that your therapist doesn't really seem to be helping you to work through the trauma, but colludes with your fear of going there, then you might consider changing your therapist. Some of your lack of progress then could be due to not working with the right therapist for your type of problems.

2.5 Effect on your family or partner

Traumas can often also have a profound effect on your partner or other members of your family or close social relationships. As outlined above, a trauma can often seem to have changed you completely from the way you were before. If you can't understand your psychological reactions to trauma, others around you can probably understand them even less so. A helpful starting point may be to share this guide with those closest to you so that they have greater understanding of what you're going through. It may be a source of great relief to those closest to you to know that what you are going through is common (given the abnormal circumstances of the trauma) and that you are not 'going mad' or 'being weak'. It may also be a relief to you to be able to be more open about the way in which you feel and what you are going through to those people closest to you in your life. Both your doctor and your therapist should be aware of the strain that reactions to trauma can cause to relationships. They may also be able to suggest ways in which your partner could be more included in the therapeutic process.

2.6 Further reading

If you would like to read a more comprehensive self-help book that gives you many more practical suggestions and exercises, you might try the book, below. This book is also written primarily for single-incident traumas (like those described in this booklet):

Overcoming Traumatic Stress- A self-help guide using Cognitive Behavioral Techniques, by Claudia Herbert and Ann Wetmore, published in 1999 by Constable & Robinson Publishing Ltd, London.**

American version, published in 2001 by New York University Press, New York

For both single-incident traumas and multiple, chronic traumas (like prolonged and repeated traumas, including childhood sexual abuse):

'I can't get over it' – A Handbook for Trauma Survivors, by Aphrodite Matsakis, Ph.D., Specialist in Post-Traumatic Stress Disorder, published in 1992 by New Harbinger Publications, Inc., Oakland, California.

Walking the Tiger – Healing Trauma, by Peter R. Levine with N. Frederick, published in 1997 by North Atlantic Books, Berkeley, California

The Body Remembers – Psychophysiology of Trauma and Trauma Treatment, by Babette Rothschild, published in 2000 by W.W. Norton & Company, New York'

Written about the impact of trauma on relationships and how to survive trauma together (mainly referring to complex trauma):

Trust after Trauma – A Guide to Relationships for Survivors and Those who Love Them, by Aphrodite Matsakis, published in 1998 by New Harbinger Publications, Oakland, California

For survivors of childhood sexual abuse:

Overcoming Childhood Trauma – A self-help guide using Cognitive Behavioral Techniques, by Helen Kennerley, published in 2000 by Constable & Robinson Ltd, London**

Breaking Free – Help for survivors of child sexual abuse, by Carolyn Ainscough & Kay Toon, (revised edition) published in 2000 by Insight, Sheldon Press, London**

Breaking Free Workbook – Practical help for survivors of child sexual abuse, by Carolyn Ainscough & Kay Toon, published in 2000 by Sheldon Press, London**

For male survivors of childhood sexual abuse:

Victims No Longer – Men Recovering from Incest and Other Sexual Child Abuse, by Mike Lew, published in 1988 by Nevraumont Publishing Co., New York.

If you want to find out how the technique of EMDR works to help trauma and to enhance performance this is an excellent book to read:

Emotional Healing at Warp Speed – The Power of EMDR (Eye Movement Desensitization and Reprocessing), by David Grand, published in 2001 by Harmony Books, New York**

For bereavement through trauma:

Living with Grief, by Tony Lake, first published in 1984 (10th edition, 2000) by Sheldon Press, London **

Grief Rituals – Tools for Healing,
by Elaine Childs-Gowell, published in 1992 by Station Hill Press, New York.

For depression:

Overcoming Depression – A self-help guide using Cognitive Behavioral Techniques, by Paul Gilbert, first published in 1997 (revised edition, 2000) by Constable & Robinson, London**

The Feeling Good Handbook, by David D. Burns, M.D., published in 1990 by Penguin Books Ltd., London.

Although most likely your anger or irritability is linked to your trauma experience, you might find some of the strategies suggested in this book helpful:

Overcoming Anger and Irritability – A self-help guide using Cognitive Behavioral Techniques, by William Davies, published in 2000 by Constable & Robinson, London**

For sexual difficulties:

For Each Other: Sharing Sexual Intimacy, by Lonnie Barbach, published in 1983 by Corgi, London.

Sexual Happiness for Women: A Practical Approach, by Maurice Yaffé and Elizabeth Fenwick, published in 1986 by Dorling Kindersley, London.

For Chronic Pain Problems you might find the following CD and Tape helpful:

Living with Chronic Pain (CD), by Neil Berry, recorded in 1999, published by Neil Berry, distributed by Blue Stallion Publications, Witney, OXON, UK**

Deep Relaxation Tapes – Coping with Everyday Stress, Side A: Encouraging Sleep; Side B: Coping with Pain, by Corinne Bennett, recorded in 1996, distributed by Blue Stallion Publications, Witney, OXON, UK**

For Relaxation and Mindful Breathing here are two tapes that you might find helpful:

Mind Balancing – Meditation & Relaxation Programme, by Reinhard Kowalski, recorded in 2001 published by The Sattva Centre, Maidenhead, UK**

The Five Minute Relaxation, by Philip Rogers, recorded in 1996 published by Living Well, UK**

All publications marked ** are obtainable via mail order (p&p free within UK) from Blue Stallion Publications, 8a Market Square, Witney, OXON OX28 6BB. Tel.: ++44 (0) 1993 77 67 87; Website: www.bluestallion.co.uk

2.7 Contact addresses

United Kingdom

1. The British Association for Behavioral and Cognitive Psychotherapies has a register of all their approved psychotherapists. Some of these specialise in working with survivors of trauma and may be able to help you.

British Association For Behavioural and Cognitive Psychotherapies (BABCP), The Globe Centre, PO Box 9, Accrington BB5 0XB
Tel: ++44 (0) 1254 875 277
Email: babcp@babcp.com
Website: www.babcp.com

2. EMDR UK and Ireland publishes a list of all their registered EMDR (Eye Movement Desensitization and Reprocessing) practitioners and consultants. If you connect to the Website of the European EMDR Association (in English), you can find a contact address for EMDR UK & Ireland and where you can get a copy of the register. There are also further information and resources on EMDR outlined.
Website: www.emdr-practitioner.net

3. The British Association for Counselling can provide you with a list of individual counsellors and counselling agencies and organizations in your local area.

British Association for Counselling and Psychotherapy (BACP)
BACP House,
15 St. John's Business Park
Lutterworth
LE17 4HB
Tel: 0870 443 5252

4. The British Psychological Society publishes a register of all approved Chartered Clinical Psychologists. These will have undergone the necessary training to be able to help you.

British Psychological Society (BPS)
St Andrews House, 48 Princess Road East, Leicester LE1 7DR
Tel: ++44 (0) 116 254 9568

5. The United Kingdom Council for Psychotherapies publishes a register of approved and qualified psychotherapists.

United Kingdom Council for Psychotherapies (UKCP)
2nd Floor, Edward House, 2 Wakley Street, London, EC1V 7LT
Tel: ++44 (0) 20 7014 9955
Email: info@psychotherapy.org.uk
Website: www.psychotherapy.org.uk

6. A private, independent trauma treatment service specializing in education, training, trauma therapy, stress management and medico-legal work.

The Oxford Stress & Trauma Centre
8a Market Square
Witney
OXON
OX28 6BB
Tel: ++44 (0) 1993 77 90 77
Website: www.oxdev.com

7. Other organizations, which it might be useful to contact:

Thought Field Therapy UK
Alexandra Healing Centre
39 Alexandria Road
West Ealing
London W13 0NR
Tel: ++44 (0) 20 8579 7230
Website: www.alexandriahealing.co.uk

8. Organizations that keep registers of qualified alternative health care practitioners:

The British Homeopathic Association
Hahnemann House
29 Park Street West
Luton LU1 3BE
Tel: 0870 444 3950

The Society of Homeopaths
11 Brookfield, Duncan Close, Moulton Park
Northampton NN3 6WL
Tel: 0845 450 6611

British Acupuncture Council
63 Jeddo Road, London, W12 9HQ
Tel: 020 8735 0400

International Society of Professional Aromatherapists
ISPA House
82 Ashby Road
Hinckley
Leicestershire LEIO 1SN
Tel: ++44 (0)1455 637 987

The Dr Edward Bach Foundation
Mount Vernoon
Sotwell
Wallingford
Oxon OX10 OPZ
Tel: ++44 (0)1491 834 678

International Register of Holistic Health Practitioners (IRHHPI)
121 Coral Street
Leicestershire
LE4 5BG

Republic of Ireland

Psychological Society of Ireland
CX House
2A Corn Exchange Place
Poolberg Street
Dublin 2
Tel: [++353] 1 671 7048

Information about Contact Addresses in the following English Speaking Countries,

AUSTRALIA
CANADA
NEW ZEALAND
SOUTH AFRICA
UNITED STATES OF AMERICA

is available on the following website: **www.oxdev.com** under Resources. It is also available on request from:

The Oxford Stress and Trauma Centre

8a Market Square

Witney

OXON OX28 6BB

Tel.: ++44 (0) 1993 77 90 77

Epilogue

Congratulations! When you have reached this part of the booklet you will have made your first steps in the process to recovery from your trauma. The first steps are to understand your reactions to the trauma. You will now know that what you are experiencing are common reactions to trauma and that you are not going mad. You will have learned that your reactions are unique to you because they are based on your experiences of the trauma and and your bodily, emotional and mental responses in trying to cope with these.

Further, you will now know that the process of recovery takes time. It will take as long as you need for it. After reading this booklet you may also find it easier to decide whether it might be helpful for you to share some of this path to recovery with a therapist, who can guide and support you in your process of healing. You will now know that this has been helpful to many people and that there is no reason to feel ashamed if you decide that professional help could be useful to you in order to regain control over your life after a trauma.

Other Titles in this Series

Self Help for Nightmares £5.50
A book for adults with frequent recurrent bad dreams
By Dr Mary Burgess, Prof. Isaac Marks, Prof. Michael Gill
First Edition 2001

Self Help for Chronic Fatigue Syndrome £6.99
A guide for young people
By Dr Trudie Chalder, Kaneez Hussain

Translation Into:

Turkish

Understanding your reactions to trauma £7.50
Deprem Sonrasi Ortaya Cikan Psikolojik Tepkiler ve Kendi Kendine
Yardim Yöntemleri
By Dr Claudia Herbert
Translated and Adapted 1999
By Dr Mehmet Zihini Sungur

Self Help for Nightmares £7.50
Kabuslar
Tekrarlayan Korkutucu Rüyalarla Basa Cikma Yöntemleri
By Dr Mary Burgess, Prof. Isaac Marks, Prof. Michael Gill
Translated and Adapted 2003
By PisikoNET Yayinlari

Self Help for Chronic Fatigue Syndrome £7.50
Kronik Yorgunluk Sendromu
Kendine Yardum Yollari
By Dr Trudie Chalder, Kaneez Hussain
Translated and Adapted 2004
By PisikoNET Yayinlari

Spanish
Understanding your reactions to trauma £7.50
Comprendiendo Las Reacciones A Los Acontecimientos Traumaticos
By Dr Claudia Herbert
Translated 2000

German
Understanding your reactions to trauma £7.50
Traumareaktionen verstehen und Hilfe finden
By Dr Claudia Herbert
Translated 2002

<u>Italian</u>
Understanding your reactions to trauma   £7.50
Capire e superare il trauma
By Dr Claudia Herbert, Dr Fabrizio Didonna
Translated and Adapted 2006
By Edizioni Erickson

<u>Polish</u>
Understanding your reactions to trauma   £7.50
Zrozumiec trauma
By Dr Claudia Herbert
Translated and Adapted 2004
By Gdanskie Wydawnictwo Psychlogiczne sp. Z.o.o.

Also Published by Blue Stallion Publications

Getting through Anxiety with CBT   £4.95
A Young Person's Guide
By Dr Ben Gurney-Smith
Series Editor: Dr Claudia Herbert

Getting through Dental Fear with CBT   £4.95
A Young Person's Guide
By Helen Chapman, Nick Kirby-Turner
Series Editor: Dr Claudia Herbert

Getting through Depression with CBT   £4.95
A Young Person's Guide
By Dr Louise Dalton, Dr Alice Farrington
Series Editor: Dr Claudia Herbert

Getting through it with CBT   £4.95
A Young Person's Guide
By Dr Claire Holdaway, Dr Nicola Connolly
Series Editor: Dr Claudia Herbert